The Ancient Mysteries and Secret Societies

Which Have Influenced Modern Masonic Symbolism

Manly Palmer Hall

Revised and Edited by
Dennis Logan

[2020]

Copyright 2020 by Rolled Scroll Publishing
ISBN: 9781952900082

The Ancient Mysteries and Secret Societies

Which Have Influenced Modern Masonic Symbolism

WHEN confronted with a problem involving the use of the reasoning faculties, individuals of strong intellect keep their poise, and seek to reach a solution by obtaining facts bearing upon the question. Those of immature mentality, on the other hand, when similarly confronted, are overwhelmed. While the former may be qualified to solve the riddle of their own destiny, the latter must be led like a flock of sheep and taught in simple language. They depend almost entirely upon the ministrations of the shepherd. The Apostle Paul said that these little ones must be fed with milk, but that meat is the food of strong men. Thought*less*ness is almost synonymous with childishness, while thought*ful*ness is symbolic of maturity.

There are, however, but few mature minds in the world; and thus it was that the philosophic-religious doctrines of the pagans were divided to meet the needs of these two fundamental groups of human intellect--one philosophic, the other incapable of appreciating the deeper mysteries of life. To the discerning few were revealed the *esoteric*, or spiritual, teachings, while the unqualified many received only the literal, or *exoteric*, interpretations. In order to make simple the great truths of Nature and the abstract principles of natural law, the vital forces of the universe were personified, becoming the gods and goddesses of the ancient mythologies. While the ignorant multitudes brought their offerings to the altars of Priapus and Pan (deities representing the procreative energies), the wise recognized in these marble statues only symbolic concretions of great abstract truths.

In all cities of the ancient world were temples for public worship and offering. In every community also were philosophers and mystics, deeply versed in Nature's lore. These individuals were usually banded together, forming seclusive philosophic and religious schools. The more important of these groups were known as the *Mysteries*. Many of the great minds of antiquity were initiated into these secret fraternities by strange and mysterious rites, some of which were extremely cruel. Alexander Wilder defines the Mysteries as "Sacred dramas performed at stated periods. The most celebrated were those of Isis, Sabazius, Cybele, and Eleusis." After being admitted, the initiates were instructed in the secret wisdom which had been preserved for ages. Plato, an initiate of one of these sacred orders, was severely criticized because in his writings he revealed to the public many of the secret philosophic principles of the Mysteries.

Every pagan nation had (and has) not only its state religion, but another into which the philosophic elect alone have gained entrance. Many of these ancient cults vanished from the earth without revealing their secrets, but a few have survived the test of ages and their mysterious symbols are still preserved. Much of the ritualism of Freemasonry is based on the trials to which candidates were subjected by the ancient hierophants before the keys of wisdom were entrusted to them.

Few realize the extent to which the ancient secret schools influenced contemporary intellects and, through those minds, posterity. Robert Macoy, 33°, in his *General History of Freemasonry*, pays a magnificent tribute to the part played by the ancient Mysteries in the rearing of the edifice of human culture. He says, in part: "It appears that all the perfection of civilization, and all the advancement made in philosophy, science, and art among the ancients are due to those institutions which, under the veil of mystery, sought to illustrate the sublimest truths of religion, morality, and virtue, and impress them on the hearts of their disciples.* * * Their chief object was to teach the doctrine of one God, the resurrection of man to eternal life, the dignity of the human soul, and to lead the people to see the shadow of the deity, in the beauty, magnificence, and splendor of the universe."

With the decline of virtue, which has preceded the destruction of every nation of history, the Mysteries became perverted. Sorcery took the place of the divine magic. Indescribable practices (such as the Bacchanalia) were introduced, and perversion ruled supreme; for no institution can be any better than the members of which it is composed. In despair, the few who were true sought to preserve the secret doctrines from oblivion. In some cases they succeeded, but more often the arcanum was lost and only the empty shell of the Mysteries remained.

Thomas Taylor has written, "Man is naturally a religious animal." From the earliest dawning of his consciousness, man has worshiped and revered *things* as symbolic of the invisible, omnipresent, indescribable *Thing*, concerning which he could discover practically nothing. The pagan Mysteries opposed the Christians during the early centuries of their church, declaring that the new faith (Christianity) did not demand virtue and integrity as requisites for salvation. Celsus expressed himself on the subject in the following caustic terms:

"That I do not, however, accuse the Christians more bitterly than truth compels, may be conjectured from hence, that the cryers who call men to other mysteries proclaim as follows: 'Let him approach whose hands are pure, and whose words are wise.' And again, others proclaim: 'Let him approach who is pure from all wickedness, whose soul is not conscious of any evil, and who leads a just and upright life.' And these things are proclaimed by those who promise a purification from error. Let us now hear who those are that are called to the Christian mysteries: Whoever is a sinner, whoever is unwise, whoever is a fool, and whoever, in short, is miserable, him the kingdom of God will receive. Do you not, therefore, call a sinner, an unjust man, a thief, a housebreaker, a wizard, one who is sacrilegious, and a robber of sepulchres? What other persons would the cryer nominate, who should call robbers together?"

It was not the true faith of the early Christian mystics that Celsus attacked, but the false forms that were creeping in even during his day. The ideals of early Christianity were based upon the high moral standards of the pagan Mysteries, and the first Christians who met under the city of Rome used as their places of worship the subterranean temples of Mithras, from whose cult has been borrowed much of the sacerdotalism of the modem church.

The ancient philosophers believed that no man could live intelligently who did not have a fundamental knowledge of Nature and her laws. Before man can obey, he must understand, and the Mysteries were devoted to instructing man concerning the operation of divine law in the terrestrial sphere. Few of the early cults actually worshiped anthropomorphic deities, although their symbolism might lead one to believe they did. They were moralistic rather than religionistic; philosophic rather than theologic. They taught man to use his faculties more intelligently, to be patient in the face of adversity, to be courageous when confronted by danger, to be true in the midst of temptation, and, most of all, to view a worthy life as the most acceptable sacrifice to God, and his body as an altar sacred to the Deity.

Sun worship played an important part in nearly all the early pagan Mysteries. This indicates the probability of their Atlantean origin, for the people of Atlantis were sun worshipers. The Solar Deity was usually personified as a beautiful youth, with long golden hair to symbolize the rays of the sun. This golden Sun God was slain by wicked ruffians, who personified the evil principle of the universe. By means of certain rituals and ceremonies, symbolic of purification and regeneration, this wonderful God of Good was brought back to life and became the Savior of His people. The secret processes whereby He was resurrected symbolized those cultures by means of which man is able to overcome his lower nature, master his appetites, and give expression to the higher side of himself. The Mysteries were

A FEMALE HIEROPHANT OF THE MYSTERIES.

From Montfaucon's *Antiquities*.

This illustration shows Cybele, here called the Syrian Goddess, in the robes of a hierophant. Montfaucon describes the figure as follows: "Upon her head is an episcopal mitre, adorned on the lower part with towers and pinnacles; over the gate of the city is a crescent, and beneath the circuit of the walls a crown of rays. The Goddess wears a sort of surplice, exactly like the surplice of a priest or bishop; and upon the surplice a tunic, which falls down to the legs; and over all an episcopal cope, with the twelve signs of the Zodiac wrought on the borders. The figure hath a lion on each side, and holds in its left hand a Tympanum, a Sistrum, a Distaff, a Caduceus, and another instrument. In her right hand she holds with her middle finger a thunderbolt, and upon the same am animals, insects, and, as far as we may guess, flowers, fruit, a bow, a quiver, a torch, and a scythe." The whereabouts of the statue is unknown, the copy reproduced by Montfaucon being from drawings by Pirro Ligorio.

organized for the purpose of assisting the struggling human creature to reawaken the spiritual powers which, surrounded by the flaming ring of lust and degeneracy, lay asleep within his soul. In other words, man was offered a way by which he could regain his lost estate. (See Wagner's *Siegfried*.)

In the ancient world, nearly all the secret societies were philosophic and religious. During the mediæval centuries, they were chiefly religious and political, although a few philosophic schools remained. In modern times, secret societies, in the Occidental countries, are largely political or fraternal, although in a few of them, as in Masonry, the ancient religious and philosophic principles still survive.

Space prohibits a detailed discussion of the secret schools. There were literally scores of these ancient cults, with branches in all parts of the Eastern and Western worlds. Some, such as those of Pythagoras and the Hermetists, show a decided Oriental influence, while the Rosicrucians, according to their own proclamations, gained much of their wisdom from Arabian mystics. Although the Mystery schools are usually associated with civilization, there is evidence that the most uncivilized peoples of prehistoric times had a knowledge of them. Natives of distant islands, many in the lowest forms of savagery, have mystic rituals and secret practices which, although primitive, are of a decided Masonic tinge.

THE DRUIDIC MYSTERIES OF BRITAIN AND GAUL

"The original and primitive inhabitants of Britain, at some remote period, revived and reformed their national institutes. Their priest, or instructor, had hitherto been simply named Gwydd, but it was considered to have become necessary to divide this office between the national, or superior, priest and another whose influence [would] be more limited. From henceforth the former became Der-Wydd (Druid), or superior instructor, and [the latter] Go-Wydd, or O-Vydd (Ovate), subordinate instructor; and both went by the general name of Beirdd (Bards), or teachers of wisdom. As the system matured and augmented, the Bardic Order consisted of three classes, the Druids, Beirdd Braint, or privileged Bards, and Ovates." (See Samuel Meyrick and Charles Smith, *The Costume of The Original Inhabitants of The British Islands*.)

The origin of the word *Druid* is under dispute. Max Müller believes that, like the Irish word *Drui*, it means "the men of the oak trees." He further draws attention to the fact that the forest gods and tree deities of the Greeks were called *dryades*. Some believe the word to be of Teutonic origin; others ascribe it to the Welsh. A few trace it to the Gaelic *druidh*, which means "a wise man" or "a sorcerer." In Sanskrit the word *dru* means "timber."

At the time of the Roman conquest, the Druids were thoroughly ensconced in Britain and Gaul. Their power over the people was unquestioned, and there were instances in which armies, about to attack each other, sheathed their swords when ordered to do so by the white-robed Druids. No undertaking of great importance was scatted without the assistance of these patriarchs, who stood as mediators between the gods and men. The Druidic Order is deservedly credited with having had a deep understanding of Nature and her laws. The *Encyclopædia Britannica* states that geography, physical science, natural theology, and astrology were their favorite studies. The Druids had a fundamental knowledge of medicine, especially the use of herbs and *simples*. Crude surgical instruments also have been found in England and Ireland. An odd treatise on early British medicine states that every practitioner was expected to have a garden or back yard for the growing of certain herbs necessary to his profession. Eliphas Levi, the celebrated transcendentalist, makes the following significant statement:

"The Druids were priests and physicians, curing by magnetism and charging amylets with their fluidic influence. Their universal remedies were mistletoe and serpents' eggs, because these substances attract the astral light in a special manner. The solemnity with which mistletoe was cut down drew upon this plant the popular confidence and rendered it powerfully magnetic. * * * The progress of magnetism will some day reveal to us the absorbing properties of mistletoe. We shall then understand the secret of those spongy growths which drew the unused virtues of plants and become surcharged with tinctures and savors. Mushrooms, truffles, gall on trees, and the different kinds of mistletoe will be employed with understanding by a medical science, which will be new because it is old * * * but one must not move quicker than science, which recedes that it may advance the further. " (See *The History of Magic.*)

Not only was the mistletoe sacred as symbolic of the universal medicine, or panacea, but also because of the fact that it grew upon the oak tree. Through the symbol of the oak, the Druids worshiped the Supreme Deity; therefore, anything growing upon that tree was sacred to Him. At certain seasons, according to the positions of the sun, moon, and stars, the Arch-Druid climbed the oak tree and cut the mistletoe with a golden sickle consecrated for that service. The parasitic growth was caught in white cloths provided for the purpose, lest it touch the earth and be polluted by terrestrial vibrations. Usually a sacrifice of a white bull was made under the tree.

The Druids were initiates of a secret school that existed in their midst. This school, which closely resembled the Bacchic and Eleusinian Mysteries of Greece or the Egyptian rites of Isis and Osiris, is justly designated the *Druidic*

Mysteries. There has been much speculation concerning the secret wisdom that the Druids claimed to possess. Their secret teachings were never written, but were communicated orally to specially prepared candidates. Robert Brown, 32°, is of the opinion that the British priests secured their information from Tyrian and Phœnician navigators who, thousands of years before the Christian Era, established colonies in Britain and Gaul while searching for tin. Thomas Maurice, in his *Indian Antiquities,* discourses at length on Phœnician, Carthaginian, and Greek expeditions to the British Isles for the purpose of procuring tin. Others are of the opinion that the Mysteries as celebrated by the Druids were of Oriental origin, possibly Buddhistic.

The proximity of the British Isles to the lost Atlantis may account for the sun worship which plays an important part in the rituals of Druidism. According to Artemidorus, Ceres and Persephone were worshiped on an island close to Britain with rites and ceremonies similar to those of Samothrace. There is no doubt that the Druidic Pantheon includes a large number of Greek and Roman deities. This greatly amazed Cæsar during his conquest of Britain and Gaul, and caused him to affirm that these tribes adored Mercury, Apollo, Mars, and Jupiter, in a manner similar to that of the Latin countries. It is almost certain that the Druidic Mysteries were not indigenous to Britain or Gaul, but migrated from one of the more ancient civilizations.

The school of the Druids was divided into three distinct parts, and the secret teachings embodied therein are practically the same as the mysteries concealed under the allegories of Blue Lodge Masonry. The lowest of the three divisions was that of Ovate (Ovydd). This was an honorary degree, requiring no special purification or preparation. The Ovates dressed in green, the Druidic color of learning, and were expected to know something about medicine, astronomy, poetry if possible, and sometimes music. An Ovate was an individual admitted to the Druidic Order because of his general excellence and superior knowledge concerning the problems of life.

The second division was that of Bard (Beirdd). Its members were robed in sky-blue, to represent harmony and truth, and to them was assigned the labor of memorizing, at least in part, the twenty thousand verses of Druidic sacred poetry. They were often pictured with the primitive British or Irish harp--an instrument strung with human hair, and having as many strings as there were ribs on one side of the human body. These Bards were often chosen as teachers of candidates seeking entrance into the Druidic Mysteries. Neophytes wore striped robes of blue, green, and white, these being the three sacred colors of the Druidic Order.

The third division was that of Druid (Derwyddon). Its particular labor was to minister to the religious needs of the people. To reach this dignity, the candidate

THE ARCH-DRUID IN HIS CEREMONIAL ROBES.

From Wellcome's *Ancient Cymric Medicine*.

The most striking adornment of the Arch-Druid was the *iodhan moran*, or breastplate of judgment, which possessed the mysterious Power of strangling any who made an untrue statement while wearing it. Godfrey Higgins states that this breastplate was put on the necks of witnesses to test the veracity of their evidence. The Druidic *tiara*, or *anguinum*, its front embossed with a number of points to represent the sun's rays, indicated that the priest was a personification of the rising sun. On the front of his belt the Arch-Druid wore the *liath meisicith*--a magic brooch, or buckle in the center of which was a large white stone. To this was attributed the power of drawing the fire of the gods down from heaven at the priest's command This specially cut stone was a burning glass, by which the sun's rays were concentrated to light the altar fires. The Druids also had other symbolic implements, such as the peculiarly shaped golden sickle with which they cut the mistletoe from the oak, and the *cornan*, or scepter, in the form of a crescent, symbolic of the sixth day of the increasing moon and also of the Ark of Noah. An early initiate of the Druidic Mysteries related that admission to their midnight ceremony was gained by means of a glass boat, called *Cwrwg Gwydrin*. This boat symbolized the moon, which, floating upon the waters of eternity, preserved the seeds of living creatures within its boatlike crescent.

must first become a Bard Braint. The Druids always dressed in white--symbolic of their purity, and the color used by them to symbolize the sun.

In order to reach the exalted position of *Arch-Druid*, or spiritual head of the organization, it was necessary for a priest to pass through the six successive degrees of the Druidic Order. (The members of the different degrees were differentiated by the colors of their sashes, for all of them wore robes of white.) Some writers are of the opinion that the title of *Arch-Druid* was hereditary, descending from father to son, but it is more probable that the honor was conferred by ballot election. Its recipient was chosen for his virtues and integrity from the most learned members of the higher Druidic degrees.

According to James Gardner, there were usually two *Arch-Druids* in Britain, one residing on the Isle of Anglesea and the other on the Isle of Man. Presumably there were others in Gaul. These dignitaries generally carried golden scepters and were crowned with wreaths of oak leaves, symbolic of their authority. The younger members of the Druidic Order were clean-shaven and modestly dressed, but the more aged had long gray beards and wore magnificent golden ornaments. The educational system of the Druids in Britain was superior to that of their colleagues on the Continent, and consequently many of the Gallic youths were sent to the Druidic colleges in Britain for their philosophical instruction and training.

Eliphas Levi states that the Druids lived in strict abstinence, studied the natural sciences, preserved the deepest secrecy, and admitted new members only after long probationary periods. Many of the priests of the order lived in buildings not unlike the monasteries of the modern world. They were associated in groups like ascetics of the Far East. Although celibacy was not demanded of them, few married. Many of the Druids retired from the world and lived as recluses in caves, in rough-stone houses, or in little shacks built in the depths of a forest. Here they prayed and medicated, emerging only to perform their religious duties.

James Freeman Clarke, in his *Ten Great Religions*, describes the beliefs of the Druids as follows: "The Druids believed in three worlds and in transmigration from one to the other: In a world above this, in which happiness predominated; a world below, of misery; and this present state. This transmigration was to punish and reward and also to purify the soul. In the present world, said they, Good and Evil are so exactly balanced that man has the utmost freedom and is able to choose or reject either. The Welsh Triads tell us there are three objects of metempsychosis: to collect into the soul the properties of all being, to acquire a knowledge of all things, and to get power to conquer evil. There are also, they say, three kinds of knowledge: knowledge of the nature of each thing, of its cause, and its influence. There are three things which continually grow less: darkness, falsehood, and death. There are three which constantly increase: light, life, and truth."

Like nearly all schools of the Mysteries, the teachings of the Druids were divided into two distinct sections. The simpler, a moral code, was taught to all the people, while the deeper, esoteric doctrine was given only to initiated priests. To be admitted to the order, a candidate was required to be of good family and of high moral character. No important secrets were intrusted to him until he had been tempted in many ways and his strength of character severely tried. The Druids taught the people of Britain and Gaul concerning the immortality of the soul. They believed in transmigration and apparently in reincarnation. They borrowed in one life, promising to pay back in the next. They believed in a purgatorial type of hell where they would be purged of their sins, afterward passing on to the happiness of unity with the gods. The Druids taught that all men would be saved, but that some must return to earth many times to learn the lessons of human life and to overcome the inherent evil of their own natures.

Before a candidate was intrusted with the secret doctrines of the Druids, he was bound with a vow of secrecy. These doctrines were imparted only in the depths of forests and in the darkness of caves. In these places, far from the haunts of men, the neophyte was instructed concerning the creation of the universe, the personalities of the gods, the laws of Nature, the secrets of occult medicine, the mysteries of the celestial bodies, and the rudiments of magic and sorcery. The Druids had a great number of feast days. The new and full moon and the sixth day of the moon were sacred periods. It is believed that initiations took place only at the two solstices and the two equinoxes. At dawn of the 25th day of December, the birth of the Sun God was celebrated.

The secret teachings of the Druids are said by some to be tinctured with Pythagorean philosophy. The Druids had a Madonna, or Virgin Mother, with a Child in her arms, who was sacred to their Mysteries; and their Sun God was resurrected at the time of the year corresponding to that at which modern Christians celebrate Easter.

Both the cross and the serpent were sacred to the Druids, who made the former by cutting off all the branches of an oak tree and fastening one of them to the main trunk in the form of the letter T. This oaken cross became symbolic of their superior Deity. They also worshiped the sun, moon, and stars. The moon received their special veneration. Caesar stated that Mercury was one of the chief deities of the Gauls. The Druids are believed to have worshiped Mercury under the similitude of a stone cube. They also had great veneration for the Nature spirits (fairies, gnomes, and undines), little creatures of the forests and rivers to whom many offerings were made.

Describing the temples of the Druids, Charles Heckethorn, in *The Secret Societies of All Ages & Countries*, says:

"Their temples wherein the sacred fire was preserved were generally situate on eminences and in dense groves of oak, and assumed various forms--circular, because a circle was the emblem of the universe; oval, in allusion to the mundane egg, from which issued, according to the traditions of many nations, the universe, or, according to others, our first parents; serpentine, because a serpent was the symbol of Hu, the Druidic Osiris; cruciform, because a cross is an emblem of regeneration; or winged, to represent the motion of the Divine Spirit. * * * Their chief deities were reducible to two--a male and a female, the great father and mother--Hu and Ceridwen, distinguished by the same characteristics as belong to Osiris and Isis, Bacchus and Ceres, or any other supreme god and goddess representing the two principles of all Being."

Godfrey Higgins states that *Hu*, the Mighty, regarded as the first settler of Britain, came from a place which the Welsh *Triads* call the Summer Country, the present site of Constantinople. Albert Pike says that the Lost Word of Masonry is concealed in the name of the Druid god *Hu*. The meager information extant concerning the secret initiations of the Druids indicates a decided similarity between their Mystery school and the schools of Greece and Egypt. *Hu*, the Sun God, was murdered and, after a number of strange ordeals and mystic rituals, was restored to life.

There were three degrees of the Druidic Mysteries, but few successfully passed them all. The candidate was buried in a coffin, as symbolic of the death of the Sun God. The supreme test, however, was being sent out to sea in an open boat. While undergoing this ordeal, many lost their lives. Taliesin, an ancient scholar, who passed through the Mysteries, describes the initiation of the open boat in Faber's *Pagan Idolatry*. The few who passed this third degree were said to have been "born again," and were instructed in the secret and hidden truths which the Druid priests had preserved from antiquity. From these initiates were chosen many of the dignitaries of the British religious and political world. (For further details, see Faber's *Pagan Idolatry*, Albert Pike's *Morals and Dogma*, and Godfrey Higgins' *Celtic Druids*.)

THE RITES OF MITHRAS

When the Persian Mysteries immigrated into Southern Europe, they were quickly assimilated by the Latin mind. The cult grew rapidly, especially among the Roman soldiery, and during the Roman wars of conquest the teachings were carried by the legionaries to nearly all parts of Europe. So powerful did the cult of Mithras become that at least one Roman Emperor was initiated into the order, which met in caverns under the city of Rome. Concerning the spread of this Mystery school through different parts of Europe, C. W. King, in his *Gnostics and Their Remains*, says:

"Mithraic bas-reliefs cut on the faces of rocks or on stone tablets still abound in the countries formerly the western provinces of the Roman Empire; many exist in Germany, still more in France, and in this island (Britain) they have often been discovered on the line of the Picts' Wall and the noted one at Bath."

Alexander Wilder, in his *Philosophy and Ethics of the Zoroasters*, states that *Mithras* is the Zend title for the sun, and he is supposed to dwell within that shining orb. Mithras has a male and a female aspect, though not himself androgynous. As Mithras, he is the ford of the sun, powerful and radiant, and most magnificent of the *Yazatas* (Izads, or Genii, of the sun). As *Mithra*, this deity represents the feminine principle; the mundane universe is recognized as her symbol. She represents Nature as receptive and terrestrial, and as fruitful only when bathed in the glory of the solar orb. The Mithraic cult is a simplification of the more elaborate teachings of Zarathustra (Zoroaster), the Persian fire magician.

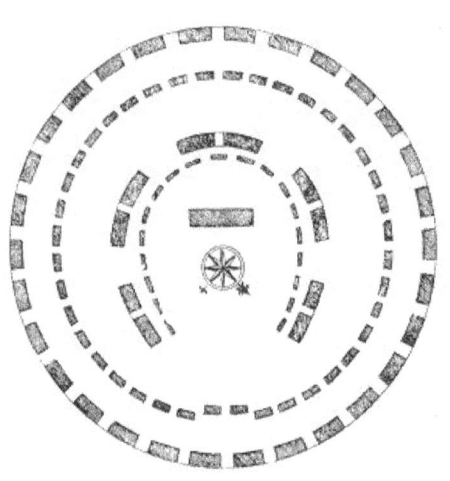

THE GROUND PLAN OF STONEHENGE.

From Maurice's *Indian Antiquities*.

The Druid temples of places of religious worship were not patterned after those of other nations. Most of their ceremonies were performed at night, either in thick groves of oak trees or around open-air altars built of great uncut stones. How these masses of rock were moved ahs not been satisfactorily explained. The most famous of their altars, a great stone ring of rocks, is Stonehenge, in Southwestern England. This structure, laid out on an astronomical basis, still stands, a wonder of antiquity.

According to the Persians, there coexisted in eternity two principles. The first of these, *Ahura-Mazda*, or *Ormuzd*, was the Spirit of Good. From Ormuzd came forth a number of hierarchies of good and beautiful spirits (angels and archangels). The second of these eternally existing principles was called *Ahriman*. He was also a pure and beautiful spirit, but he later rebelled against Ormuzd, being jealous of his power. This did not occur, however, until after Ormuzd had created light, for previously Ahriman had not been conscious of the existence of Ormuzd. Because of his jealousy and rebellion, Ahriman became the Spirit of Evil. From himself he individualized a host of destructive creatures to injure Ormuzd.

When Ormuzd created the earth, Ahriman entered into its grosser elements. Whenever Ormuzd did a good deed, Ahriman placed the principle of evil within it. At last when Ormuzd created the human race, Ahriman became incarnate in the lower nature of man so that in each personality the Spirit of

Good and the Spirit of Evil struggle for control. For 3,000 years Ormuzd ruled the celestial worlds with light and goodness. Then he created man. For another 3,000 years he ruled man with wisdom, and integrity. Then the power of Ahriman began, and the struggle for the soul of man continues through the next period of 3,000 years. During the fourth period of 3,000 years, the power of Ahriman will be destroyed. Good will return to the world again, evil and death will be vanquished, and at last the Spirit of Evil will bow humbly before the throne of Ormuzd. While Ormuzd and Ahriman are struggling for control of the human soul and for supremacy in Nature, Mithras, God of Intelligence, stands as mediator between the two. Many authors have noted the similarity between mercury and Mithras. As the chemical mercury acts as a solvent (according to alchemists), so Mithras seeks to harmonize the two celestial opposites.

There are many points of resemblance between Christianity and the cult of Mithras. One of the reasons for this probably is that the Persian mystics invaded Italy during the first century after Christ and the early history of both cults was closely interwoven. The Encyclopædia Britannica makes the following statement concerning the Mithraic and Christian Mysteries:

"The fraternal and democratic spirit of the first communities, and their humble origin; the identification of the object of adoration with light and the sun; the legends of the shepherds with their gifts and adoration, the flood, and the ark; the representation in art of the fiery chariot, the drawing of water from the rock; the use of bell and candle, holy water and the communion; the sanctification of Sunday and of the 25th of December; the insistence on moral conduct, the emphasis placed on abstinence and self-control; the doctrine of heaven and hell, of primitive revelation, of the mediation of the Logos emanating from the divine, the atoning sacrifice, the constant warfare between good and evil and the final triumph of the former, the immortality of the soul, the last judgment, the resurrection of the flesh and the fiery destruction of the universe--[these] are some of the resemblances which, whether real or only apparent, enabled Mithraism to prolong its resistance to Christianity,"

The rites of Mithras were performed in caves. Porphyry, in his *Cave of the Nymphs*, states that Zarathustra (Zoroaster) was the first to consecrate a cave to the worship of God, because a cavern was symbolic of the earth, or the lower world of darkness. John P. Lundy, in his *Monumental Christianity*, describes the cave of Mithras as follows:

"But this cave was adorned with the signs of the zodiac, Cancer and Capricorn. The summer and winter solstices were chiefly conspicuous, as the gates of souls descending into this life, or passing out of it in their ascent to the Gods; Cancer being the gate of descent, and Capricorn of ascent. These are the two avenues of the immortals passing up and down from earth to heaven, and from heaven to earth."

The so-called chair of St. Peter, in Rome, was believed to have been used in one of the pagan Mysteries, possibly that of Mithras, in whose subterranean grottoes the votaries of the Christian Mysteries met in the early days of their faith. In *Anacalypsis*, Godfrey Higgins writes that in 1662, while cleaning this sacred chair of Bar-Jonas, the Twelve Labors of Hercules were discovered upon it, and that later the French discovered upon the same chair the Mohammedan confession of faith, written in Arabic.

Initiation into the rites of Mithras, like initiation into many other ancient schools of philosophy, apparently consisted of three important degrees. Preparation for these degrees consisted of self-purification, the building up of the intellectual powers, and the control of the animal nature. In the first degree the candidate was given a crown upon the point of a sword and instructed in the mysteries of Mithras' hidden power. Probably he was taught that the golden crown represented his own spiritual nature, which must be objectified and unfolded before he could truly glorify Mithras; for Mithras was his own soul, standing as mediator between Ormuzd, his spirit, and Ahriman, his animal nature. In the second degree he was given the armor of intelligence and purity and sent into the darkness of subterranean pits to fight the beasts of lust, passion, and degeneracy. In the third degree he was given a cape, upon which were drawn or woven the signs of the zodiac and other astronomical symbols. After his initiations were over, he was hailed as one who had risen from the dead, was instructed in the secret teachings of the Persian mystics, and became a full-fledged member of the order. Candidates who successfully passed the Mithraic initiations were

MITHRAS SLAYING THE BULL.

From Lundy's *Monumental Christianity*.

The most famous sculpturings and reliefs of this prototokos show Mithras kneeling upon the recumbent form of a great bull, into whose throat he is driving a sword. The slaying of the bull signifies that the rays of the sun, symbolized by the sword, release at the vernal equinox the vital essences of the earth--the blood of the bull--which, pouring from the wound made by the Sun God, fertilize the seeds of living things. Dogs were held sacred to the cult of Mithras, being symbolic of sincerity and trustworthiness. The Mithraics used the serpent a an emblem of Ahriman, the Spirit of Evil, and water rats were held sacred to him. The bull is esoterically the Constellation of Taurus; the serpent, its opposite in the zodiac, Scorpio; the sun, Mithras, entering into the side of the bull, slays the celestial creature and nourishes the universe with its blood.

called *Lions* and were marked upon their foreheads with the Egyptian cross. Mithras himself is often pictured with the head of a lion and two pairs of wings. Throughout the entire ritual were repeated references to the birth of Mithras as the Sun God, his sacrifice for man, his death that men might have eternal life, and lastly, his resurrection and the saving of all humanity by his intercession before the throne of Ormuzd. (See Heckethorn.)

THE BIRTH OF MITHRAS.

From Montfaucon's Antiquities

Mithras was born out of a rock, which, breaking open, permitted him to emerge. This occurred in the darkness of a subterranean chamber. The Church of the Nativity at Bethlehem confirms the theory that Jesus was born in a grotto, or cave. According to Dupuis, Mithras was put to death by crucifixion and rose again on the third day.

While the cult of Mithras did not reach the philosophic heights attained by Zarathustra, its effect upon the civilization of the Western world was far-reaching, for at one time nearly all Europe was converted to its doctrines. Rome, in her intercourse with other nations, inoculated them with her religious principles; and many later institutions have exhibited Mithraic culture. The reference to the "Lion" and the "Grip of the Lion's Paw" in the Master Mason's degree have a strong Mithraic tinge and may easily have originated from this cult. A ladder of seven rungs appears in the Mithraic initiation. Faber is of the opinion that this ladder was originally a pyramid of seven steps. It is possible that the Masonic ladder with seven rungs had its origin in this Mithraic symbol. Women were never permitted to enter the Mithraic Order, but children of the male sex were initiates long before they reached maturity. The refusal to permit women to join the Masonic Order may be based on the esoteric reason given in the secret instructions of the Mithraics. This cult is another excellent example of those secret societies whose legends are largely symbolic representations of the sun and his journey through the houses of the heavens. Mithras, rising from a stone, is merely the sun rising over the horizon, or, as the ancients supposed, out of the horizon, at the vernal equinox.

John O'Neill disputes the theory that Mithras was intended as a solar deity. In *The Night of the Gods* he writes: "The Avestan Mithra, the yazata of light, has '10,000 eyes, high, with full knowledge (perethuvaedayana), strong, sleepless and ever awake (jaghaurvaunghem).'The supreme god Ahura Mazda also has one Eye, or else it is said that 'with his eyes, the sun, moon and stars, he sees everything.' The theory that Mithra was *originally* a title of the supreme heavens-god--putting the sun out of court--is the only one that answers all requirements. It will be evident that here we have origins in abundance for the Freemason's Eye and 'its nunquam dormio.'" The reader must nor confuse the Persian Mithra with the Vedic Mitra. According to Alexander Wilder, "The Mithraic rites superseded the Mysteries of Bacchus, and became the foundation of the Gnostic system, which for many centuries prevailed in Asia, Egypt, and even the remote West."

THE MYSTERIES OF GNOSTICISM

THE entire history of Christian and pagan Gnosticism is shrouded in the deepest mystery and obscurity; for, while the Gnostics were undoubtedly prolific writers, little of their literature has survived. They brought down upon themselves the animosity of the early Christian Church, and when this institution reached its position of world power it destroyed all available records of the Gnostic *cultus*. The name *Gnostic* means *wisdom*, or *knowledge*, and is derived from the Greek *Gnosis*. The members of the order claimed to be familiar with the secret doctrines of early Christianity. They interpreted the Christian Mysteries according to pagan symbolism. Their secret information and philosophic tenets they concealed from the profane and taught to a small group only of especially initiated persons.

Simon Magus, the magician of New Testament fame, is often supposed to have been the founder of Gnosticism. If this be true, the sect was formed during the century after Christ and is probably the first of the many branches which have sprung from the main trunk of Christianity. Everything with which the enthusiasts of the early Christian Church might not agree they declared to be inspired by the Devil. That Simon Magus had mysterious and supernatural powers is conceded even by his enemies, but they maintained that these powers were lent to him by the infernal spirits and furies which they asserted were his ever present companions. Undoubtedly the most interesting legend concerning Simon is that which tells of his theosophic contests with the Apostle Peter while the two were promulgating their differing doctrines in

THE DEATH OF SIMON THE MAGICIAN.

From the *Nuremberg Chronicle*.

Simon Magus, having called upon the Spirits of the Air, is here shown being picked up by the demons. St. Peter demands that the evil genii release their hold upon the magician. The demons are forced to comply and Simon Magus is killed by the fall.

Rome. According to the story that the Church Fathers have preserved, Simon was to prove his spiritual superiority by ascending to heaven in a chariot of fire. He was actually picked up and carried many feet into the air by invisible powers. When St. Peter saw this, he cried out in a loud voice, ordering the demons (spirits of the air) to release their hold upon the magician. The evil spirits, when so ordered by the great saint, were forced to obey. Simon fell a great distance and was killed, which decisively proved the superiority of the Christian powers. This story is undoubtedly manufactured out of whole cloth, as it is only one out of many accounts concerning his death, few of which agree. As more and more evidence is being amassed to the effect that St, Peter was never in Rome, its last possible vestige of authenticity is rapidly being dissipated.

That Simon was a philosopher there is no doubt, for wherever his exact words are preserved his synthetic and transcending thoughts are beautifully expressed. The principles of Gnosticism are well described in the following verbatim statement by him, supposed to have been preserved by Hippolytus: "To you, therefore, I say what I say, and write what I write. And the writing is this. Of the universal Æons [periods, planes, or cycles of creative and created life in substance and space, celestial creatures] there are two shoots, without beginning or end, springing from one Root, which is the power invisible, inapprehensible silence [Bythos]. Of these shoots one is manifested from above, which is the Great Power, the Universal Mind ordering all things, male, and the other, [is manifested] from below, the Great Thought, female, producing all things. Hence pairing with each other, they unite and manifest the Middle Distance, incomprehensible Air, without beginning or end. In this is the Father Who sustains all things, and nourishes those things which have a beginning and end." (See *Simon Magus*, by G. R. S. Mead.) By this we are to understand that manifestation is the result of a positive and a negative principle, one acting upon the other, and it takes place in the middle plane, or point of equilibrium, called the *pleroma*. This *pleroma* is a peculiar substance produced out of the blending of the spiritual and material æons. Out of the *pleroma* was individualized the *Demiurgus*, the immortal mortal, to whom we are responsible for our physical existence and the suffering we must go through in connection with it. In the Gnostic system, three pairs of opposites, called *Syzygies*, emanated from the Eternal One. These, with Himself, make the total of seven. The six (three pairs) Æons (living, divine principles) were described by Simon in the *Philosophumena* in the following manner: The first two were *Mind* (Nous) and *Thought* (Epinoia). Then came *Voice* (Phone) and its opposite, *Name* (Onoma), and lastly, *Reason* (Logismos) and *Reflection* (Enthumesis). From these primordial six, united with the *Eternal Flame*, came forth the Æons (Angels) who formed the lower worlds through the direction of the Demiurgus. (See the works of H. P. Blavatsky.) How this first Gnosticism of Simon Magus and Menander, his disciple, was amplified, and frequently distorted, by later adherents to the cult must now be considered.

The School of Gnosticism was divided into two major parts, commonly called the Syrian Cult and the Alexandrian Cult. These schools agreed in essentials, but the latter division was more inclined to be pantheistic, while the former was dualistic. While the Syrian cult was largely Simonian, the Alexandrian School was the outgrowth of the philosophical deductions of a clever Egyptian Christian, Basilides by name, who claimed to have received his instructions from the Apostle Matthew. Like Simon Magus, he was an emanationist, with Neo-Platonic inclinations. In fact, the entire Gnostic Mystery is based upon the hypothesis of emanations as being the logical connection between the irreconcilable opposites Absolute Spirit and Absolute Substance, which the Gnostics believed to have been coexistent in Eternity.

Some assert that Basilides was the true founder of Gnosticism, but there is much evidence to the effect that Simon Magus laid down its fundamental principles in the preceding century.

The Alexandrian Basilides inculcated Egyptian Hermeticism, Oriental occultism, Chaldean astrology, and Persian philosophy in his followers, and in his doctrines sought to unite the schools of early Christianity with the ancient pagan Mysteries. To him is attributed the formulation of that peculiar concept of the Deity which carries the name of Abraxas. In discussing the original meaning of this word, Godfrey Higgins, in his Celtic Druids, has demonstrated that the numerological powers of the letters forming the word Abraxas when added together result in the sum of 365. The same author also notes that the name Mithras when treated in a similar manner has the same numerical value. Basilides caught that the powers of the universe were divided into 365 Æons, or spiritual cycles, and that the sum of all these together was the Supreme Father, and to Him he gave the Qabbalistical appellation *Abraxas*, as being symbolical, numerologically, of His divine powers, attributes, and emanations. *Abraxas* is usually symbolized as a composite creature, with the body of a human being and the head of a rooster, and with each of his legs ending in a serpent. C. W. King, in his *Gnostics and Their Remains*, gives the following concise description of the Gnostic philosophy of Basilides, quoting from the writings of the early Christian bishop and martyr, St. Irenæus: "He asserted that God, the uncreated, eternal Father, had first brought forth Nous, or Mind; this the Logos, Word; this again Phronesis, Intelligence; from Phronesis sprung Sophia, Wisdom, and Dynamis, Strength."

In describing Abraxas, C. W. King says: "Bellermann considers the composite image, inscribed with the actual name Abraxas, to be a Gnostic Pantheos, representing the Supreme Being, with the Five Emanations marked out by appropriate symbols. From the human body, the usual form assigned to the Deity, spring the two supporters, Nous and Logos, expressed in the serpents, symbols of the inner senses, and the quickening understanding; on which account the Greeks had made the serpent the attribute of Pallas. His head--that of a cock--represents Phronesis, that bird being the emblem of foresight and of vigilance. His two arms hold the symbols of Sophia and Dynamis: the shield of Wisdom and the whip of Power."

The Gnostics were divided in their opinions concerning the Demiurgus, or creator of the lower worlds. He established the terrestrial universe with the aid of six sons, or emanations (possibly the planetary Angels) which He formed out of, and yet within, Himself. As stated before, the Demiurgus was individualized as the lowest creation out of the substance called *pleroma*. One group of the Gnostics was of the opinion that the Demiurgus was the cause of all misery and was an evil creature, who by building this lower world had separated the souls of men from truth by encasing them in mortal vehicles. The other sect viewed the Demiurgus as being divinely inspired and merely fulfilling the dictates of the invisible Lord. Some Gnostics were of the opinion that the Jewish God, *Jehovah*, was the Demiurgus. This concept, under a slightly different name, apparently influenced mediæval Rosicrucianism, which viewed Jehovah as the Lord of the material universe rather than as the Supreme Deity. Mythology abounds with the stories of gods who partook of both celestial and terrestrial natures. Odin, of Scandinavia, is a good example of a deity subject to mortality, bowing before the laws of Nature and yet being, in certain senses at least, a Supreme Deity.

The Gnostic viewpoint concerning the Christ is well worthy of consideration. This order claimed to be the only sect to have actual pictures of the Divine

Syrian. While these were, in all probability, idealistic conceptions of the Savior based upon existing sculpturings and paintings of the pagan sun gods, they were all Christianity had. To the Gnostics, the Christ was the personification of *Nous*, the Divine Mind, and emanated from the higher spiritual Æons. He descended into the body of Jesus at the baptism and left it again before the crucifixion. The Gnostics declared that the Christ was not crucified, as this Divine *Nous* could not suffer death, but that Simon, the Cyrenian, offered his life instead and that the *Nous*, by means of its power, caused Simon to resemble Jesus. Irenæus makes the following statement concerning the cosmic sacrifice of the Christ:

"When the uncreated, unnamed Father saw the corruption of mankind, He sent His firstborn, Nous, into the world, in the form of Christ, for the redemption of all who believe in Him, out of the power of those that have fabricated the world (the Demiurgus, and his six sons, the planetary genii). He appeared amongst men as the Man Jesus, and wrought miracles." (See King's *Gnostics and Their Remains*.)

The Gnostics divided humanity into three parts: those who, as savages, worshiped only the visible Nature; those who, like the Jews, worshiped the Demiurgus; and lastly, themselves, or others of a similar cult, including certain sects of Christians, who worshiped *Nous* (Christ) and the true spiritual light of the higher Æons.

After the death of Basilides, Valentinus became the leading inspiration of the Gnostic movement. He still further complicated the system of Gnostic philosophy by adding infinitely to the details. He increased the number of emanations from the Great One (the Abyss) to fifteen pairs and also laid much emphasis on the *Virgin Sophia*, or Wisdom. In the *Books of the Savior*, parts of which are commonly known as the *Pistis Sophia*, may be found much material concerning this strange doctrine of Æons and their strange inhabitants. James Freeman Clarke, in speaking of the doctrines of the Gnostics, says: "These doctrines, strange as they seem to us, had a wide influence in the Christian Church." Many of the theories of the ancient Gnostics, especially those concerning scientific subjects, have been substantiated by modern research. Several sects branched off from the main stem of Gnosticism, such as the Valentinians, the Ophites (serpent worshipers), and the Adamites. After the third century their power waned, and the Gnostics practically vanished from the philosophic world. An effort was made during the Middle Ages to resurrect the principles of Gnosticism, but owing to the destruction of their records the material necessary was not available. Even today there are evidences of Gnostic philosophy in the modern world, but they bear other names and their true origin is not suspected. Many of the Gnostic concepts have actually been incorporated into the dogmas of the Christian Church, and our newer interpretations of Christianity are often along the lines of Gnostic emanationism.

THE MYSTERIES OF , ASAR-HAPI

The identity of the Greco-Egyptian Serapis (known to the Greeks as *Serapis* and the Egyptians as *Asar-Hapi*) is shrouded by an impenetrable veil of mystery. While this deity was a familiar figure among the symbols of the secret Egyptian initiatory rites, his arcane nature was revealed only to those who had fulfilled the requirements of the Serapic cultus. Therefore, in all probability, excepting the initiated priests, the Egyptians themselves were ignorant of his true character. So far as known, there exists no authentic account of the rites of Serapis, but an analysis of the deity and his accompanying symbols reveals their salient points. In an oracle delivered to the King of Cyprus, Serapis described himself thus:

"A god I am such as I show to thee,
The Starry Heavens are my head, my trunk the sea,
Earth forms my feet, mine ears the air supplies,
The Sun's far-darting, brilliant rays, mine eyes."

Several unsatisfactory attempts have been made to etymologize the word *Serapis*. Godfrey Higgins notes that *Soros* was the name given by the Egyptians to a stone coffin, and *Apis* was Osiris incarnate in the sacred bull. These two words combined result in *Soros-Apis* or *Sor-Apis*, "the tomb of the bull." But it is improbable that the Egyptians would worship a coffin in the form of a man.

Several ancient authors, including Macrobius, have affirmed that Serapis was a name for the Sun, because his image so often had a halo of light about its head. In his *Oration Upon the Sovereign Sun*, Julian speaks of the deity in these words: "One Jove, one Pluto, one Sun is Serapis." In Hebrew, Serapis is *Saraph*, meaning "to blaze out" or "to blaze up." For this reason the Jews designated one of their hierarchies of spiritual beings, *Seraphim*.

The most common theory, however, regarding the origin of the name *Serapis* is that which traces its derivation from the compound *Osiris-Apis*. At one time the Egyptians believed that the dead were absorbed into the nature of Osiris, the god of the dead. While marked similarity exists between Osiris-Apis and Serapis, the theory advanced by Egyptologists that Serapis is merely a name given to the dead Apis, or sacred bull of Egypt, is untenable in view of the transcendent wisdom possessed by the Egyptian priestcraft, who, in all probability, used the god to symbolize the soul of the world (*anima mundi*). The material body of Nature was called *Apis*; the soul which escaped from the body at death but was enmeshed with the form during physical life was designated *Serapis*.

C. W. King believes Serapis to be a deity of Brahmanic extraction, his name being the Grecianized form of *Ser-adah* or *Sri-pa*, two titles ascribed to *Yama*, the Hindu god of death. This appears reasonable, especially since there is a legend to the effect that Serapis, in the form of a bull, was driven by Bacchus from India to Egypt. The priority of the Hindu Mysteries would further substantiate such a theory.

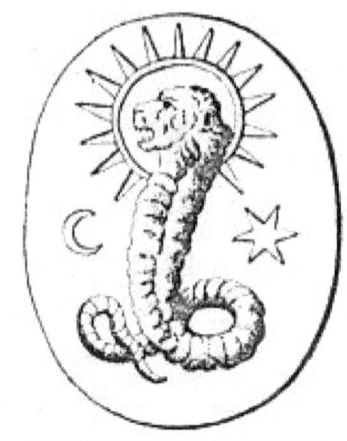

THE LION-FACED LIGHT-POWER.

From *Montfaucon's Antiquities*.

This Gnostic gem represents by its serpentine body the pathway of the Sun and by its lion head the exaltation of the solar in the constellation of Leo.

Among other meanings suggested for the word *Serapis* are: "The Sacred Bull," "The Sun in Taurus," "The Soul of Osiris," "The Sacred Serpent," and "The Retiring of the Bull." The last appellation has reference to the ceremony of drowning the sacred Apis in the waters of the Nile every twenty-five years.

There is considerable evidence that the famous statue of Serapis in the Serapeum at Alexandria was originally worshiped under another name at Sinope, from which it was brought to Alexandria. There is also a legend which tells that Serapis was a very early king of the Egyptians, to whom they owed the foundation of their philosophical and scientific power. After his death this king was elevated to the estate of a god. Phylarchus declared that the word *Serapis* means "the power that disposed the universe into its present beautiful order."

In his *Isis and Osiris*, Plutarch gives the following account of the origin of the magnificent statue of Serapis which stood in the Serapeum at Alexandria:

THE ALEXANDRIAN SERAPIS.

From Mosaize *Historie der Hebreeuwse Kerke*.

Serapis is often shown standing on the back of the sacred crocodile, carrying in his left hand a rule with which to measure the inundations of the Nile, and balancing with his right hand a curious emblem consisting of an animal with three heads. The first head--that of a lion--signified the present; the second head--that of a wolf--the past; and the third head--that of a dog--the future. The body with its three heads was enveloped by the twisted coils of a serpent. Figures of Serapis are occasionally accompanied by Cerberus, the three-headed dog of Pluto, and--like Jupiter--carry baskets of grain upon their heads.

While he was Pharaoh of Egypt, Ptolemy Soter had a strange dream in which he beheld a tremendous statue, which came to life and ordered the Pharaoh to bring it to Alexandria with all possible speed. Ptolemy Soter, not knowing the whereabouts of the statue, was sorely perplexed as to how he could discover it. While the Pharaoh was relating his dream, a great traveler by the name of Sosibius, coming forward, declared that he had seen such an image at Sinope. The Pharaoh immediately dispatched Soteles and Dionysius to negotiate for the removal of the figure to Alexandria. Three years elapsed before the image was finally obtained, the representatives of the Pharaoh finally stealing it and concealing the theft by spreading a story that the statue had come to life and, walking down the street leading from its temple, had boarded the ship prepared for its transportation to Alexandria. Upon its arrival in Egypt, the figure was brought into the presence of two Egyptian Initiates--the Eumolpid Timotheus and Manetho the Sebennite--who, immediately pronounced it to be Serapis. The priests then declared that it was equipollent to Pluto. This was a masterly stroke, for in Serapis the Greeks and Egyptians found a deity in common and thus religious unity was consummated between the two nations.

Several figures of Serapis that stood in his various temples in Egypt and Rome have been described by early authors. Nearly all these showed Grecian rather than Egyptian influence. In some the body of the god was encircled by the coils of a great serpent. Others showed him as a composite of Osiris and Apis.

A description of the god that in all probability is reasonably accurate is that which represents him as a tall, powerful figure, conveying the twofold impression of manly strength and womanly grace. His face portrayed a deeply pensive mood, the expression inclining toward sadness. His hair was long and arranged in a somewhat feminine manner, resting in curls upon his breast and shoulders. The face, save for its heavy beard, was also decidedly feminine. The figure of Serapis was usually robed from head to foot in heavy draperies, believed by initiates to conceal the fact that his body was androgynous.

Various substances were used in making the statues of Serapis. Some undoubtedly were carved from stone or marble by skilled craftsmen; others may have been cast from base or precious metals. One colossus of Serapis was composed of plates of various metals fitted together. In a labyrinth sacred to Serapis stood a thirteen-foot statue of him reputed to have been made from a single emerald. Modern writers, discussing this image, state that it was made of green glass poured into a mold. According to the Egyptians, however, it withstood all the tests of an actual emerald.

Clement of Alexandria describes a figure of Serapis compounded from the following elements: First, filings of gold, silver, lead, and tin; second, all manner of Egyptian stones, including sapphires, hematites, emeralds, and topazes; all these being ground down and mixed together with the coloring matter left over from the funeral of Osiris and Apis. The result was a rare and curious figure, indigo in color. Some of the statues of Serapis must have been formed of extremely hard substances, for when a Christian soldier, carrying out the edict of Theodosius, struck the Alexandrian Serapis with his ax, that instrument was shattered into fragments and sparks flew from it. It is also quite probable that Serapis was worshiped in the form of a serpent, in common with many of the higher deities of the Egyptian and Greek pantheons.

Serapis was called *Theon Heptagrammaton*, or the god with the name of seven letters. The name *Serapis* (like Abraxas and Mithras) contains seven letters. In their hymns to Serapis the priests chanted the seven vowels. Occasionally Serapis is depicted with horns or a coronet of seven rays. These evidently represented the seven divine intelligences manifesting through the solar light. The *Encyclopædia Britannica* notes that the earliest authentic mention of Serapis is in connection with the death of Alexander. Such was the prestige of Serapis that he alone of the gods was consulted in behalf of the dying king.

The Egyptian secret school of philosophy was divided into the Lesser and the Greater Mysteries, the former being sacred to Isis and the latter to Serapis and Osiris. Wilkinson is of the opinion that only the priests were permitted to enter the Greater Mysteries. Even the heir to the throne was not eligible until he had been crowned Pharaoh, when, by virtue of his kingly office, he automatically became a priest and the temporal head of the state religion. (See Wilkinson's *Manners and Customs of the Egyptians*.) A limited number were admitted into the Greater Mysteries: these preserved their secrets inviolate.

Much of the information concerning the rituals of the higher degrees of the Egyptian Mysteries has been gleaned from an examination of the chambers and passageways in which the initiations were given. Under the temple of Serapis destroyed by Theodosius were found strange mechanical contrivances constructed by the priests in the subterranean crypts and caverns where the nocturnal initiatory rites were celebrated. These machines indicate the severe tests of moral and physical courage undergone by the candidates. After passing through these tortuous ways, the neophytes who Survived the ordeals were ushered into the presence of Serapis, a noble and awe-inspiring figure illumined by unseen lights.

A SYMBOLIC LABYRINTH.

From *Montfaucon's Antiquities*.

Labyrinths were also a striking feature in connection with the Rice of Serapis, and E. A. Wallis Budge, in his *Gods of the Egyptians*, depicts Serapis(Minotaur-like) with the body of a man and the head of a bull. Labyrinths were symbolic of the involvements and illusions of the lower world through which wanders the soul of man in its search for truth. In the labyrinth

Labyrinths and mazes were favored places of initiation among many ancient cults. Remains of these mystic mazes have been found among the American Indians, Hindus, Persians, Egyptians, and Greeks. Some of these mazes are merely involved pathways lined with stones; others are literally miles of gloomy caverns under temples or hollowed from the sides of mountains. The famous labyrinth of Crete, in which roamed the bull-headed Minotaur, was unquestionably a place of initiation into the Cretan Mysteries.

dwells the lower animal man with the head of the bull, who seeks to destroy the soul entangled in the maze of worldly ignorance. In this relation Serapis becomes the Tryer or Adversary who tests the souls of those seeking union with the Immortals. The maze was also doubtless used to represent the solar system, the Bull-Man representing the sun dwelling in the mystic maze of its planets, moons, and asteroids.

The Gnostic Mysteries were acquainted with the arcane meaning of Serapis, and through the medium of Gnosticism this god became inextricably associated with early Christianity. In fact, the Emperor Hadrian, while traveling in Egypt in A.D. 24, declared in a letter to Servianus that the worshipers of Serapis were Christians and that the Bishops of the church also worshiped at his shrine. He even declared that the Patriarch himself, when in Egypt, was forced to adore Serapis as well as Christ. (See Parsons' *New Light on the Great Pyramid*.)

The little-suspected importance of Serapis as a prototype of Christ can be best appreciated after a consideration of the following extract from C. W. King's *Gnostics and Their Remains*: "There can be no doubt that the head of Serapis, marked as the face is by a grave and pensive majesty, supplied the first idea for the conventional portraits of the Saviour. The Jewish prejudices of the first converts were so powerful that we may be sure no attempt was made to depict His countenance until some generations after all that had beheld it on earth had passed away."

Serapis gradually usurped the positions previously occupied by the other Egyptian and Greek gods, and became the supreme deity of both religions. His power continued until the fourth century of the Christian Era. In A.D. 385, Theodosius, that would-be exterminator of pagan philosophy, issued his memorable edict *De Idolo Serapidis Diruendo*. When the Christian soldiers, in obedience to this order, entered the Serapeum at Alexandria to destroy the image of Serapis which had stood there for centuries, so great was their veneration for the god that they dared not touch the image lest the ground should open at their feet and engulf them. At length, overcoming their fear, they demolished the statue, sacked the building, and finally as a fitting climax to their offense burned the magnificent library which was housed within the lofty apartments of the Serapeum. Several writers have recorded the remarkable fact that Christian symbols were found in the ruined foundations of this pagan temple. Socrates, a church historian of the fifth century, declared that after the pious Christians had razed the Serapeum at Alexandria and scattered the demons who dwelt there under the guise of gods, beneath the foundations was found the monogram of Christ!

Two quotations will further establish the relationship existing between the Mysteries of Serapis and those of other ancient peoples. The first is from Richard Payne Knight's *Symbolical Language of Ancient Art and Mythology*: "Hence Varro [in *De Lingua Latina*] says that Cœlum and Terra, that is universal mind and productive body, were the Great Gods of the Samothracian Mysteries; and the same as the Serapis and Isis of the later Ægyptians: the Taautos and Astarte of the Phœnicians, and the Saturn and Ops of the Latins." The second quotation is from Albert Pike's *Morals and Dogma*: "'Thee,' says Martianus Capella, in his hymn to the Sun, 'dwellers on the Nile adore as Serapis, and Memphis worships as Osiris: in the sacred rites of Persia thou art Mithras, in Phrygia, Atys, and Libya bows down to thee as Ammon, and Phœnician Byblos as Adonis; thus the whole world adores thee under different names.'"

THE ODINIC MYSTERIES

The date of the founding of the Odinic Mysteries is uncertain, some writers declaring that they were established in the first century before Christ; others, the first century after Christ. Robert Macoy, 33°, gives the following description of their origin: "It appears from the northern chronicles that in the first century of the Christian Era, Sigge, the chief of the Aser, an Asiatic tribe, emigrated from the Caspian sea and the Caucasus into northern Europe. He directed his course northwesterly from the Black sea to Russia, over which, according to tradition, he placed one of his sons as a ruler, as he is said to have done over the Saxons and the Franks. He then advanced through Cimbria to Denmark, which acknowledged his fifth son Skiold as its sovereign, and passed over to Sweden, where Gylf, who did homage to the wonderful stranger, and was initiated into his mysteries, then ruled. He soon made himself master here, built Sigtuna as the capital of his empire, and promulgated a new code of laws, and established the sacred mysteries. He, himself, assumed the name of Odin, founded the priesthood of the twelve Drottars (Druids?) who conducted the secret worship, and the administration of justice, and, as prophets, revealed the future. The secret rites of these mysteries celebrated the death of Balder, the beautiful and lovely, and represented the grief of Gods and men at his death, and his restoration to life." (*General History of Freemasonry*.)

After his death, the historical Odin was apotheosized, his identity being merged into that of the mythological Odin, god of wisdom, whose cult he had promulgated. Odinism then supplanted the worship of Thor, the thunderer, the supreme deity of the ancient Scandinavian pantheon. The mound where, according to legend, King Odin was buried is still to be seen near the site of his great temple at Upsala.

The twelve *Drottars* who presided over the Odinic Mysteries evidently personified the twelve holy and ineffable names of Odin. The rituals of the Odinic Mysteries were very similar to those of the Greeks, Persians, and Brahmins, after which they were patterned. The Drottars, who symbolized the signs of the zodiac, were the custodians of the arts and sciences, which they revealed to those who passed successfully the ordeals of initiation. Like many other pagan cults, the Odinic Mysteries, as an institution, were destroyed by Christianity, but the underlying cause of their fall was the corruption of the priesthood.

Mythology is nearly always the ritual and the symbolism of a Mystery school. Briefly stated, the sacred drama which formed the basis of the Odinic Mysteries was as follows:

The Supreme, invisible Creator of all things was called All-Father. His regent in Nature was Odin, the one-eyed god. Like Quetzalcoatl, Odin was elevated to the dignity of the Supreme Deity. According to the Drottars, the universe was fashioned from the body of *Ymir*, the hoarfrost giant. Ymir was formed from the clouds of mist that rose from Ginnungagap, the great cleft in chaos into which the primordial frost giants and flame giants had hurled snow and fire. The three gods--Odin, Vili, and Ve--slew Ymir and from him formed the world. From Ymir's various members the different parts of Nature were fashioned.

After Odin had established order, he caused a wonderful palace, called Asgard, to be built on the top of a mountain, and here the twelve Æsir (gods) dwelt together, far above the limitations of mortal men. On this mountain also was Valhalla, the palace of the slain, where those who had heroically died fought and feasted day after day. Each night their wounds were healed and the boar whose flesh they ate renewed itself as rapidly as it was consumed.

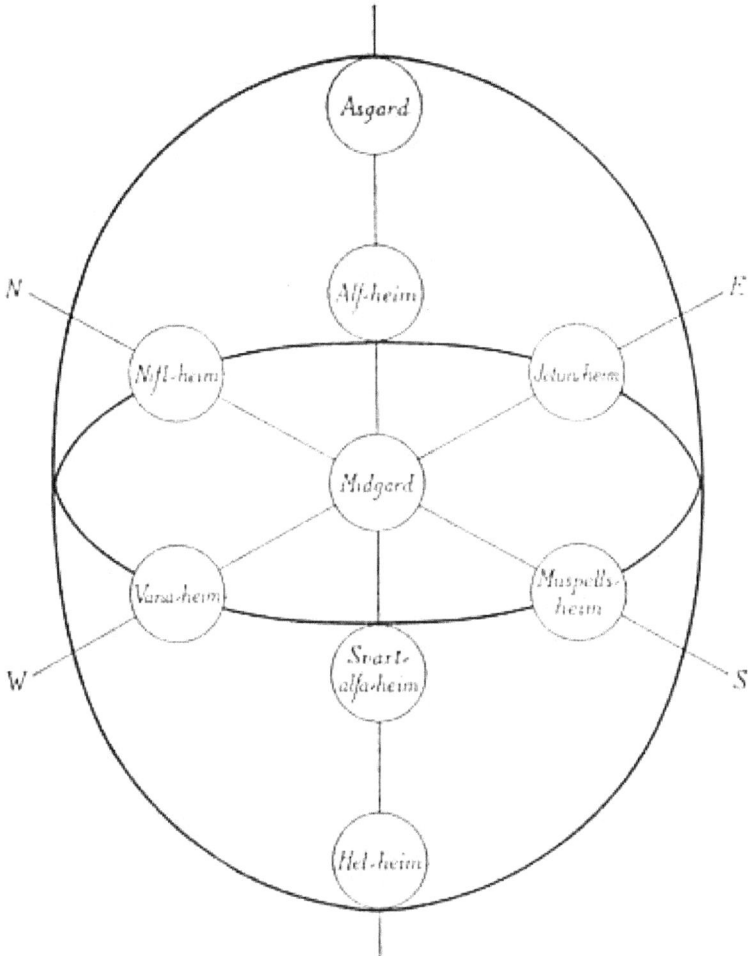

THE NINE WORLDS OF THE ODINIC MYSTERIES.

The Nordic Mysteries were given in nine chambers, or caverns, the candidate advancing through them in sequential order. These chambers of initiation represented the nine spheres into which the Drottars divided the universe: (1) *Asgard*, the Heaven World of the Gods; (2) *Alf-heim*, the World of the light and beautiful Elves, or Spirits; (3) *Nifl-heim*, the World of Cold and Darkness, which is located in the North; (4) *Jotun-heim*, the World of the Giants, which is located in the East; (5) *Midgard*, the Earth World of human beings, which is located in the midst, or middle place; (6) *Vana-heim*, the World of the Vanes, which is located in the West; (7) *Muspells-heim*, the World of Fire, which is located in the South; 8) *Svart-alfa-heim*, the World of the dark and treacherous Elves, which is under the earth; and (9) *Hel-heim*, the World of cold and the abode of the dead, which is located at the very lowest point of the universe. It is to be understood that all of these worlds are invisible to the senses, except Midgard, the home of human creatures, but during the process of initiation the soul of the candidate--liberated from its earthly sheath by the secret power of the priests--wanders amidst the inhabitants of these various spheres. There is undoubtedly a relationship between the nine worlds of the Scandinavians and the nine spheres, or planes, through which initiates of the Eleusinian Mysteries passed in their ritual of regeneration.

Balder the Beautiful--the Scandinavian Christ--was the beloved son of Odin. Balder was not warlike; his kindly and beautiful spirit brought peace and joy to the hearts of the gods, and they all loved him save one. As Jesus had a Judas among His twelve disciples, so one of the twelve gods was false--Loki, the personification of evil. Loki caused Höthr, the blind god of fate, to shoot Balder with a mistletoe arrow. With the death of Balder, light and joy vanished from the lives of the other deities. Heartbroken, the gods gathered to find a method whereby they could resurrect this spirit of eternal life and youth. The result was the establishment of the Mysteries.

The Odinic Mysteries were given in underground crypts or caves, the chambers, nine in number, representing the Nine Worlds of the Mysteries. The candidate seeking admission was assigned the task of raising Balder from the dead. Although he did not realize it, he himself played the part of Balder. He called himself a wanderer; the caverns through which he passed were symbolic of the worlds and spheres of Nature. The priests who initiated him were emblematic of the sun, the moon, and the stars. The three supreme initiators--the Sublime, the Equal to the Sublime, and the Highest--were analogous to the Worshipful Master and the junior and Senior Wardens of a Masonic lodge.

After wandering for hours through the intricate passageways, the candidate was ushered into the presence of a statue of Balder the Beautiful, the prototype of all initiates into the Mysteries. This figure stood in the center of a great apartment roofed with shields. In the midst of the chamber stood a plant with seven blossoms, emblematic of the planers. In this room, which symbolized the house of the Æsir, or Wisdom, the neophyte took his oath of secrecy and piety upon the naked blade of a sword. He drank the sanctified mead from a bowl made of a human skull and, having passed successfully through all the tortures and trials designed to divert him from the course of wisdom, he was finally permitted to unveil the mystery of Odin--the personification of wisdom. He was presented, in the name of Balder, with the sacred ring of the order; he was hailed as a man reborn; and it was said of him that he had died and had been raised again without passing through the gates of death.

Richard Wagner's immortal composition, *Der Ring des Nibelungen*, is based upon the Mystery rituals of the Odinic cult. While the great composer took many liberties with the original story, the Ring Operas, declared to be the grandest tetralogy of music dramas the world possesses, have caught and preserved in a remarkable manner the majesty and power of the original sagas. Beginning with *Das Rheingold*, the action proceeds through *Die Walküre* and *Siegfried* to an awe-inspiring climax in *Götterdämmerung*, "The Twilight of the Gods."

THE ELEUSINIAN MYSTERIES

THE most famous of the ancient religious Mysteries were the Eleusinian, whose rites were celebrated every five years in the city of Eleusis to honor Ceres (Demeter, Rhea, or Isis) and her daughter, Persephone. The initiates of the Eleusinian School were famous throughout Greece for the beauty of their philosophic concepts and the high standards of morality which they demonstrated in their daily lives. Because of their excellence, these Mysteries spread to Rome and Britain, and later the initiations were given in both these countries. The Eleusinian Mysteries, named for the community in Attica where the sacred dramas were first presented, are generally believed to have been founded by Eumolpos about fourteen hundred years before the birth of Christ, and through the Platonic system of philosophy their principles have been preserved to modern times.

The rites of Eleusis, with their Mystic interpretations of Nature's most precious secrets, overshadowed the civilizations of their time and gradually absorbed many smaller schools, incorporating into their own system whatever valuable information these lesser institutions possessed. Heckethorn sees in the Mysteries of Ceres and Bacchus a metamorphosis of the rites of Isis and Osiris, and there is every reason to believe that all so-called secret schools of the ancient world were branches from one philosophic tree which, with its root in heaven and its branches on the earth, is--like the spirit of man--an invisible but ever-present cause of the objectified vehicles that give it expression. The Mysteries were the channels through which this one philosophic light was disseminated, and their initiates, resplendent with intellectual and spiritual understanding, were the perfect fruitage of the divine tree, bearing witness before the material world of the recondite source of all Light and Truth.

The rites of Eleusis were divided into what were called the Lesser and the Greater Mysteries. According to James Gardner, the Lesser Mysteries were celebrated in the spring (probably at the time of the vernal equinox) in the town of Agræ, and the Greater, in the fall (the time of the autumnal equinox) at Eleusis or Athens. It is supposed that the former were given annually and the latter every five years. The rituals of the Eleusinians were highly involved, and to understand them required a deep study of Greek mythology, which they interpreted in its esoteric light with the aid of their secret keys.

The Lesser Mysteries were dedicated to Persephone. In his *Eleusinian and Bacchic Mysteries*, Thomas Taylor sums up their purpose as follows: "The Lesser Mysteries were designed by the ancient theologists, their founders, to signify occultly the condition of the unpurified soul invested with an earthy body, and enveloped in a material and physical nature."

The legend used in the Lesser rites is that of the abduction of the goddess Persephone, the daughter of Ceres, by Pluto, the lord of the underworld, or Hades. While Persephone is picking flowers in a beautiful meadow, the earth suddenly opens and the gloomy lord of death, riding in a magnificent chariot, emerges from its somber depths and, grasping her in his arms, carries the screaming and struggling goddess to his subterranean palace, where he forces her to become his queen.

It is doubtful whether many of the initiates themselves understood the mystic meaning of this allegory, for most of them apparently believed that it referred solely to the succession of the seasons. It is difficult to obtain satisfactory information concerning the Mysteries, for the candidates were bound by inviolable oaths never to reveal their inner secrets to the profane. At the beginning of the ceremony of initiation, the candidate stood upon the skins of animals sacrificed for the purpose, and vowed that death should seal his lips before he would divulge the sacred truths which were about to be communicated to him. Through indirect channels, however, some of their secrets have been preserved. The teachings given to the neophytes were substantially as follows:

The soul of man--often called *Psyche*, and in the Eleusinian Mysteries symbolized by Persephone--is essentially a spiritual thing. Its true home is in the higher worlds, where, free from the bondage of material form and material concepts, it is said to be truly alive and self-expressive. The human, or physical, nature of man, according to this doctrine, is a tomb, a quagmire, a false and impermanent thing, the source of all sorrow and suffering. Plato describes the body as the sepulcher of the soul; and by this he means not only the human form but also the human nature.

The gloom and depression of the Lesser Mysteries represented the agony of the spiritual soul unable to express itself because it has accepted the limitations and illusions of the human environment. The crux of the Eleusinian argument was that man is neither better nor wiser after death than during life. If he does not rise above ignorance during his sojourn here, man goes at death into eternity to wander about forever, making the same mistakes which he made here. If he does not outgrow the desire for material possessions here, he will carry it with him into the invisible world, where, because he can never gratify the desire, he will continue in endless agony. Dante's *Inferno* is symbolically descriptive of the sufferings of those who never freed their spiritual natures from the cravings, habits, viewpoints, and limitations of their Plutonic personalities. Those who made no endeavor to improve themselves (whose souls have slept) during their physical lives, passed at death into Hades, where, lying in rows, they slept through all eternity as they had slept through life.

To the Eleusinian philosophers, birch into the physical world was death in the fullest sense of the word, and the only true birth was that of the spiritual soul of man rising out of the womb of his own fleshly nature. "The soul is dead that slumbers," says Longfellow, and in this he strikes the keynote of the Eleusinian Mysteries. Just as Narcissus, gazing at himself in the water (the ancients used this mobile element to symbolize the transitory, illusionary, material universe) lost his life trying to embrace a reflection, so man, gazing into the mirror of Nature and accepting as his real self the senseless clay that he sees reflected, loses the opportunity afforded by physical life to unfold his immortal, invisible Self.

An ancient initiate once said that the living are ruled by the dead. Only those conversant with the Eleusinian concept of life could understand that statement. It means that the majority of people are not ruled by their living spirits but by their senseless (hence dead) animal personalities. Transmigration and reincarnation were taught in these Mysteries, but in a somewhat unusual manner. It was believed that at midnight the invisible worlds were closest to the Terrestrial sphere and that souls coming into material existence slipped in during the midnight hour. For this reason many of the Eleusinian ceremonies were performed at midnight. Some of those sleeping spirits who had failed to awaken their higher natures during the earth life and who now floated around in the invisible worlds, surrounded by a darkness of their own making, occasionally slipped through at this hour and assumed the forms of various creatures.

The mystics of Eleusis also laid stress upon the evil of suicide, explaining that there was a profound mystery concerning this crime of which they could not speak, but warning their disciples that a great sorrow comes to all who take their own lives. This, in substance, constitutes the esoteric doctrine given to the initiates of the Lesser Mysteries. As the degree dealt largely with the miseries of those who failed to make the best use of their philosophic opportunities, the chambers of initiation were subterranean and the horrors of Hades were vividly depicted in a complicated ritualistic drama. After passing successfully through the tortuous passageways, with their trials and dangers, the candidate received the honorary title of *Mystes*. This meant one who saw through a veil or had a clouded vision. It also signified that the candidate had been brought up to the veil, which would be torn away in the higher degree. The modern word *mystic*, as referring to a seeker after truth according to the dictates of the heart along the path of faith, is probably derived from this ancient word, for faith is belief in the reality of things unseen or veiled.

The Greater Mysteries (into which the candidate was admitted only after he had successfully passed through the ordeals of the Lesser, and not always then) were sacred to Ceres, the mother of Persephone, and represent her as wandering through the world in quest of her abducted daughter. Ceres carried two torches, intuition and reason, to aid her in the search for her lost child (the soul). At last she found Persephone not far from Eleusis, and out of gratitude taught the people there to cultivate corn, which is sacred to her. She also founded the Mysteries. Ceres appeared before Pluto, god of the souls of the dead, and pleaded with him to allow Persephone to return to her home. This the god at first refused to do, because Persephone had eaten of the pomegranate, the fruit of mortality. At last, however, he compromised and agreed to permit Persephone to live in the upper world half of the year if she would stay with him in the darkness of Hades for the remaining half.

The Greeks believed that Persephone was a manifestation of the solar energy, which in the winter months lived under the earth with Pluto, but in the summer returned again with the goddess of productiveness. There is a legend that the flowers loved Persephone and that every year when she left for the dark realms of Pluto, the plants and shrubs would die of grief. While the profane and uninitiated had their own opinions on these subjects, the truths of the Greek allegories remained safely concealed by the priests, who alone recognized the sublimity of these great philosophic and religious parables.

Thomas Taylor epitomizes the doctrines of the Greater Mysteries in the following statement: "The Greater (Mysteries) obscurely intimated, by mystic and splendid visions, the felicity of the soul both here and hereafter when purified from the defilement of a material nature, and constantly elevated to the realities of intellectual (spiritual) vision."

THE RAPE OF PERSEPHONE.

From Thomassin's *Recucil des Figures, Groupes, Themes, Fontaines, Vases et autres Ornements*.

Pluto, the lord of the underworld, represents the body intelligence of man; and the rape of Persephone is symbolic of the divine nature assaulted and defiled by the animal soul and dragged downward into the somber darkness of Hades, which is here used as a synonym for the material, or objective, sphere of consciousness.

In his *Disquisitions upon the Painted Greek Vases*, James Christie presents Meursius' version of the occurrences taking place during the nine days required for the enactment of the Greater Eleusinian Rites. The first day was that of general meeting, during which those to be initiated were questioned concerning their several qualifications. The second day was spent in a procession to the sea, possibly for the submerging of a image of the presiding goddess. The third day was opened by the sacrifice of a mullet. On the fourth day the mystic basket containing certain sacred symbols was brought to Eleusis, accompanied by a number of female devotees carrying smaller baskets. On the evening of the fifth day there was a torch race, on the sixth a procession led by a statue of Iacchus, and on the seventh an athletic contest. The eighth day was devoted to a repetition of the ceremonial for the benefit of any who might have been prevented from coming sooner. The ninth and last day was devoted to the deepest philosophical issues of the Eleusinia, during which an urn or jar--the symbol of Bacchus--was exhibited as an emblem of supreme importance.

Just as the Lesser Mysteries discussed the prenatal epoch of man when the consciousness in its nine days (embryologically, months) was descending into the realm of illusion and assuming the veil of unreality, so the Greater Mysteries discussed the principles of spiritual regeneration and revealed to initiates not only the simplest but also the most direct and complete method of liberating their higher natures from the bondage of material ignorance. Like Prometheus chained to the top of Mount Caucasus, man's higher nature is chained to his inadequate personality. The nine days of initiation were also symbolic of the nine spheres through which the human soul descends during the process of assuming a terrestrial form. The secret exercises for spiritual unfoldment given to disciples of the higher degrees are unknown, but there is every reason to believe that they were similar to the Brahmanic Mysteries, since it is known that the Eleusinian ceremonies were closed with the Sanskrit words "Konx Om Pax."

That part of the allegory referring to the two six-month periods during one of which Persephone must remain with Pluto, while during the other she may revisit the upper world, offers material for deep consideration. It is probable that the Eleusinians realized that the soul left the body during steep, or at least was made capable of leaving by the special training which undoubtedly they were in a position to give. Thus Persephone would remain as the queen of Pluto's realm during the waking hours, but would ascend to the spiritual worlds during the periods of sleep. The initiate was taught how to intercede with Pluto to permit Persephone (the initiate's soul) to ascend from the darkness of his material nature into the light of understanding. When thus freed from the shackles of clay and crystallized concepts, the initiate was liberated not only for the period of his life but for all eternity, for never thereafter was he divested of those soul qualities which after death were his vehicles for manifestation and expression in the so-called heaven world.

In contrast to the idea of Hades as a state of darkness below, the gods were said to inhabit the tops of mountains, a well-known example being Mount Olympus, where the twelve deities of the Greek pantheon were said to dwell together. In his initiatory wanderings the neophyte therefore entered chambers of ever-increasing brilliancy to portray the ascent of the spirit from the lower worlds into the realms of bliss. As the climax to such wanderings he entered a great vaulted room, in the center of which stood a brilliantly illumined statue of the goddess Ceres. Here, in the presence of the hierophant and surrounded by priests in magnificent robes, he was instructed in the highest of the secret mysteries of the Eleusis. At the conclusion of this ceremony he was hailed as an *Epoptes*, which means one who has beheld or seen directly. For this reason also initiation was termed *autopsy*. The Epoptes was then given certain sacred books, probably written in cipher, together with tablets of stone on which secret instructions were engraved.

In *The Obelisk in Freemasonry,* John A. Weisse describes the officiating personages of the Eleusinian Mysteries as consisting of a male and a female hierophant who directed the initiations; a male and a female torchbearer; a male herald; and a male and a female altar attendant. There were also numerous minor officials. He states that, according to Porphyry, the hierophant represents Plato's *Demiurgus*, or Creator of the world; the torch bearer, the Sun; the altar man, the Moon; the herald, Hermes, or Mercury; and the other officials, minor stars.

From the records available, a number of strange and apparently supernatural phenomena accompanied the rituals. Many initiates claim to have actually seen the living gods themselves. Whether this was the result of religious ecstasy or the actual cooperation of invisible powers with the visible priests must remain a mystery. In *The Metamorphosis, or Golden Ass,* Apuleius thus describes what in all probability is his initiation into the Eleusinian Mysteries:

"I approached to the confines of death, and having trod on the threshold of Proserpine I, returned from it, being carried through all the elements. At midnight I saw the sun shining with a splendid light; and I manifestly drew near to, the gods beneath, and the gods above, and proximately adored them."

CERES, THE PATRON OF THE MYSTERIES.

From a mural painting in Pompeii.

Ceres, or Demeter, was the daughter of Kronos and Rhea, and by Zeus the mother of Persephone. Some believe her to be the goddess of the earth, but more correctly she is the deity protecting agriculture in general and corn in particular. The Poppy is sacred to Ceres and she is often shown carrying or ornamented by a garland of these flowers. In the Mysteries, Ceres represented riding in a chariot drawn by winged serpents.

Women and children were admitted to the Eleusinian Mysteries, and at one time there were literally thousands of initiates. Because this vast host was not prepared for the highest spiritual and mystical doctrines, a division necessarily took place within the society itself. The higher teachings were given to only a limited number of initiates who, because of superior mentality, showed a comprehensive grasp of their underlying philosophical concepts. Socrates refused to be initiated into the Eleusinian Mysteries, for knowing its principles without being a member of the order he realized that membership would seal his tongue. That the Mysteries of Eleusis were based upon great and eternal truths is attested by the veneration in which they were held by the great minds of the ancient world. M. Ouvaroff asks, "Would Pindar, Plato, Cicero, Epictetus, have spoken of them with such admiration, if the hierophant had satisfied himself with loudly proclaiming his own opinions, or those of his order?"

The garments in which candidates were initiated were preserved for many years and were believed to possess almost sacred properties. Just as the soul can have no covering save wisdom and virtue, so the candidates--being as yet without true knowledge--were presented to the Mysteries unclothed, being first: given the skin of an animal and later a consecrated robe to symbolize the philosophical teachings received by the initiate. During the course of initiation the passed through two gates. The first led downward into the lower worlds and symbolized his birth into ignorance. The second led upward into a room brilliantly lighted by unseen lamps, in which was the statue of Ceres and which symbolized the upper world, or the abode of Light and Truth. Strabo states that the great temple of Eleusis would hold between twenty and thirty thousand people. The caves dedicated by Zarathustra also had these two doors, symbolizing the avenues of birth and death.

THE PROCESSIONAL OF THE BACCHIC RITES.

From Ovid's *Metamorphosis*.

In the initiation, of the Bacchic Mysteries, the rôle of Bacchus is played by the candidate who, set upon by priests in the guise of the Titans, is slain and finally restored to life amidst great rejoicing. The Bacchic Mysteries were given every three years, and like the Eleusinian Mysteries, were divided into two degrees. The initiates were crowned with myrtle and ivy, plants which were sacred to Bacchus.

In the *Anacalypsis*, Godfrey Higgins conclusively establishes Bacchus (Dionysos) as one of the early pagan forms of the Christos myth, "The birthplace of Bacchus, called Sabazius or Sabaoth, was claimed by several places in Greece; but on Mount Zelmisus, in Thrace, his worship seems to have been chiefly celebrated. He was born of a virgin on the 25th of December; he performed great miracles for the good of mankind; particularly one in which he changed water into wine; he rode in a triumphal procession on an ass; he was put to death by the Titans, and rose again from the dead on the 25th of March: he was always called the Saviour. In his mysteries, he was shown to the people, as an infant is by the Christians at this day, on Christmas Day morning in Rome."

While Apollo most generally represents the sun, Bacchus is also a form of solar energy, for his resurrection was accomplished with the assistance of Apollo. The resurrection of Bacchus signifies merely the extraction or disentanglement of the various Parts of the Bacchic constitution from the Titanic constitution of the world. This is symbolized by the smoke or soot rising from the burned bodies of the Titans. The soul is symbolized by smoke because it is extracted by the fire of the Mysteries. Smoke signifies the ascension of the soul, far evolution is the process of the soul rising, like smoke, from the divinely consumed material mass. At me time the Bacchic Rites were of a high order, but later they became much degraded . The Bacchanalia, or orgies of Bacchus, are famous in literature.

The following paragraph from Porphyry gives a fairly adequate conception of Eleusinian symbolism: "God being a luminous principle, residing in the midst of the most subtile fire, he remains for ever invisible to the eyes of those who do not elevate themselves above material life: on this account, the sight of transparent bodies, such as crystal, Parian marble, and even ivory, recalls the idea of divine light; as the sight of gold excites an idea of its purity, for gold cannot he sullied. Some have thought by a black stone was signified the invisibility of the divine essence. To express supreme reason, the Divinity was represented under the human form--and beautiful, for God is the source of beauty; of different ages, and in various attitudes, sitting or upright; of one or the other sex, as a virgin or a young man, a husband or a bride, that all the shades and gradations might be marked. Every thing luminous was subsequently attributed to the gods; the sphere, and all that is spherical, to the universe, to the sun and the moon--sometimes to Fortune and to Hope. The circle, and all circular figures, to eternity--to the celestial movements; to the circles and zones of the heavens. The section of circles, to the phases of the moon; and pyramids and obelisks, to the igneous principle, and through that to the gods of Heaven. A cone expresses the sun, a cylinder the earth; the phallus and triangle (a symbol of the matrix) designate generation." (From *Essay on the Mysteries of Eleusis* by M. Ouvaroff.)

The Eleusinian Mysteries, according to Heckethorn, survived all others and did not cease to exist as an institution until nearly four hundred years after Christ, when they were finally suppressed by Theodosius (styled the Great), who cruelly destroyed all who did not accept the Christian faith. Of this greatest of all philosophical institutions Cicero said that it taught men not only how to live but also how to die.

THE ORPHIC MYSTERIES

Orpheus, the Thracian bard, the great initiator of the Greeks, ceased to be known as a man and was celebrated as a divinity several centuries before the Christian Era. "As to Orpheus himself * * *, " writes Thomas Taylor, "scarcely a vestige of his life is to be found amongst the immense ruins of time. For who has ever been able to affirm any thing with certainty of his origin, his age, his country, and condition? This alone may be depended on, from general assent, that there formerly lived a person named Orpheus, who was the founder of theology among the Greeks; the institutor of their lives and morals; the first of prophets, and the prince of poets; himself the offspring of a Muse; who taught the Greeks their sacred rites and mysteries, and from whose wisdom, as from a perennial and abundant fountain, the divine muse of Homer and the sublime theology of Pythagoras and Plato flowed." (See *The Mystical Hymns of Orpheus*.)

Orpheus was founder of the Grecian mythological system which he used as the medium for the promulgation of his philosophical doctrines. The origin of his philosophy is uncertain. He may have got it from the Brahmins, there being legends to the effect that he got it was a Hindu, his name possibly being derived from ὀρφανῖος, meaning "dark." Orpheus was initiated into the Egyptian Mysteries, from which he secured extensive knowledge of magic, astrology, sorcery, and medicine. The Mysteries of the Cabiri at Samothrace were also conferred upon him, and these undoubtedly contributed to his knowledge of medicine and music.

The romance of Orpheus and Eurydice is one of the tragic episodes of Greek mythology and apparently constitutes the outstanding feature of the Orphic Rite. Eurydice, in her attempt to escape from a villain seeking to seduce her, died from the venom of a poisonous serpent which stung her in the heel. Orpheus, penetrating to the very heart of the underworld, so charmed Pluto and Persephone with the beauty of his music that they agreed to permit Eurydice to return to life if Orpheus could lead her back to the sphere of the living without once looking round to see if she were following. So great was his fear, however, that she would stray from him that he turned his head, and Eurydice with a heartbroken cry was swept back into the land of death.

Orpheus wandered the earth for a while disconsolate, and there are several conflicting accounts of the manner of his death. Some declare that he was slain by a bolt of lightning; others, that failing to save his beloved Eurydice, he committed suicide. The generally accepted version of his death, however, is that he was torn to pieces by Ciconian women whose advances he had spurned. In the tenth book of Plato's *Republic* it is declared that, because of his sad fate at the hands of women, the soul that had once been Orpheus, upon being destined to live again in the physical world, chose rather to return in the body of a swan than be born of woman. The head of Orpheus, after being torn from his body, was cast with his lyre into the river Hebrus, down which it floated to the sea, where, wedging in a cleft in a rock, it gave oracles for many years. The lyre, after being stolen from its shrine and working the destruction of the thief, was picked up by the gods and fashioned into a constellation.

Orpheus has long been sung as the patron of music. On his seven-stringed lyre he played such perfect harmonies that the gods themselves were moved to acclaim his power. When he touched the strings of his instrument the birds and beasts gathered about him, and as he wandered through the forests his enchanting melodies caused even the ancient trees with mighty effort to draw their gnarled roots from out the earth and follow him. Orpheus is one of the many Immortals who have sacrificed themselves that mankind might have the wisdom of the gods. By the symbolism of his music he communicated the divine secrets to humanity, and several authors have declared that the gods, though loving him, feared that he would overthrow their kingdom and therefore reluctantly encompassed his destruction.

As time passed on the historical Orpheus became hopelessly confounded with the doctrine he represented and eventually became the symbol of the Greek school of the ancient wisdom. Thus Orpheus was declared to be the son of Apollo, the divine and perfect truth, and Calliope, the Muse of harmony and rhythm. In other words, Orpheus is the secret doctrine (Apollo) revealed through music (Calliope). Eurydice is humanity dead from the sting of the serpent of false knowledge and imprisoned in the underworld of ignorance. In this allegory Orpheus signifies theology, which wins her from the king of the dead but fails to accomplish her resurrection because it falsely estimates and mistrusts the innate understanding within the human soul. The Ciconian women who tore Orpheus limb from limb symbolize the various contending theological factions which destroy the body of Truth. They cannot accomplish this, however, until their discordant cries drown out the harmony drawn by Orpheus from his magic lyre. The head of Orpheus signifies the esoteric doctrines of his cult. These doctrines continue to live and speak even after his body (the cult) has been destroyed. The lyre is the secret teaching of Orpheus; the seven strings are the seven divine truths which are the keys to universal knowledge. The differing accounts of his death represent the various means used to destroy the secret teachings: wisdom can die in many ways at the same time. The allegory of Orpheus incarnating in the white swan merely signifies that the spiritual truths he promulgated will continue and will be taught by the illumined initiates of all future ages. The swan is the symbol of the initiates of the Mysteries; it is a symbol also of the divine power which is the progenitor of the world.

THE BACCHIC AND DIONYSIAC RITES

The Bacchic Rite centers around the allegory of the youthful Bacchus (Dionysos or Zagreus) being torn to pieces by the Titans. These giants accomplished the destruction of Bacchus by causing him to become fascinated by his own image in a mirror. After dismembering him, the Titans first boiled the pieces in water and afterwards roasted them. Pallas rescued the heart of the murdered god, and by this precaution Bacchus (Dionysos) was enabled to spring forth again in all his former glory. Jupiter, the Demiurgus, beholding the crime of the Titans, hurled his thunderbolts and slew them, burning their bodies to ashes with heavenly fire. Our of the ashes of the Titans--which also contained a portion of the flesh of Bacchus, whose body they had partly devoured--the human race was created. Thus the mundane life of every man was said to contain a portion of the Bacchic life.

For this reason the Greek Mysteries warned against suicide. He who attempts to destroy himself raises his hand against the nature of Bacchus within him, since man's body is indirectly the tomb of this god and consequently must be preserved with the greatest care.

Bacchus (Dionysos) represents the rational soul of the inferior world. He is the chief of the Titans--the artificers of the mundane spheres. The Pythagoreans called him the *Titanic monad*. Thus Bacchus is the all-inclusive idea of the Titanic sphere and the Titans--or *gods of the fragments*--the active agencies by means of which universal substance is fashioned into the pattern of this idea. The Bacchic state signifies the unity of the rational soul in a state of self-knowledge, and the Titanic state the diversity of the rational soul which, being scattered throughout creation, loses the consciousness of its own essential one-ness. The mirror into which Bacchus gazes and which is the cause of his fall is the great sea of illusion--the lower world fashioned by the Titans. Bacchus (the mundane rational soul), seeing his image before him, accepts the image as a likeness of himself and ensouls the likeness; that is, the rational idea ensouls its reflection--the irrational universe. By ensouling the irrational image it implants in it the urge to become like its source, the rational image. Therefore the ancients said that man does not know the gods by logic or by reason but rather by realizing the presence of the gods within himself.

After Bacchus gazed into the mirror and followed his own reflection into matter, the rational soul of the world was broken up and distributed by the Titans throughout the mundane sphere of which it is the essential nature, but the heart, or source, of it they could not: scatter. The Titans took the dismembered body of Bacchus and boiled it in water--symbol of immersion in the material universe--which represents the incorporation of the Bacchic principle in form. The pieces were afterwards roasted to signify the subsequent ascension of the spiritual nature out of form.

When Jupiter, the father of Bacchus and the Demiurgus of the universe, saw that the Titans were hopelessly involving the rational or divine idea by scattering its members through the constituent parts of the lower world, he slew the Titans in order that the divine idea might not be entirely lost. From the ashes of the Titans he formed mankind, whose purpose of existence was to preserve and eventually to release the Bacchic idea, or rational soul, from the Titanic fabrication. Jupiter, being the Demiurgus and fabricator of the material universe, is the third person of the Creative Triad, consequently the Lord of Death, for death exists only in the lower sphere of being over which he presides. Disintegration takes place so that reintegration may follow upon a higher level of form or intelligence. The thunderbolts of Jupiter are emblematic of his disintegrative power; they reveal the purpose of death, which is to rescue the rational soul from the devouring power of the irrational nature.

Man is a composite creature, his lower nature consisting of the fragments of the Titans and his higher nature the sacred, immortal flesh (life) of Bacchus. Therefore man is capable of either a Titanic (irrational) or a Bacchic (rational) existence. The Titans of Hesiod, who were twelve in number, are probably analogous to the celestial zodiac, whereas the Titans who murdered and dismembered Bacchus represent the zodiacal powers distorted by their involvement in the material world. Thus Bacchus represents the sun who is dismembered by the signs of the zodiac and from whose body the universe is formed. When the terrestrial forms were created from the various parts of his body the sense of wholeness was lost and the sense of separateness established. The heart of Bacchus, which was saved by Pallas, or Minerva, was lifted out of the four elements symbolized by his dismembered body and placed in the ether. The heart of Bacchus is the immortal center of the rational soul.

After the rational soul had been distributed throughout creation and the nature of man, the Bacchic Mysteries were instituted for the purpose of disentangling it from the irrational Titanic nature. This disentanglement was the process of lifting the soul out of the state of separateness into that of unity. The various parts and members of Bacchus were collected from the different corners of the earth. When all the rational parts are gathered Bacchus is resurrected.

The Rites of Dionysos were very similar to those of Bacchus, and by many these two gods are considered as one. Statues of Dionysos were carried in the Eleusinian Mysteries, especially the lesser degrees. Bacchus, representing the soul of the mundane sphere, was capable of an infinite multiplicity of form and designations. Dionysos apparently was his solar aspect.

The Dionysiac Architects constituted an ancient secret society, in principles and doctrines much like the modern Freemasonic Order. They were an organization of builders bound together by their secret knowledge of the relationship between the earthly and the divine sciences of architectonics. They were supposedly employed by King Solomon in the building of his Temple, although they were not Jews, nor did they worship the God of the Jews, being followers of Bacchus and Dionysos. The Dionysiac Architects erected many of the great monuments of antiquity. They possessed a secret language and a system of marking their stones. They had annual convocations and sacred feasts. The exact nature of their doctrines is unknown. It is believed that CHiram Abiff was an initiate of this society.

www.ingramcontent.com/pod-product-compliance
Lightning Source LLC
Chambersburg PA
CBHW061512040426
42450CB00008B/1584